D1395605

Man
Points

1 3 5 7 9 10 8 6 4 2

Ebury Press, an imprint of Ebury Publishing
20 Vauxhall Bridge Road, London SW1V 2SA

Ebury Press is part of the Penguin Random House group of companies
whose addresses can be found at global.penguinrandomhouse.com

Penguin
Random House
UK

www.eburypublishing.co.uk

A CIP catalogue record for this book is available from the British Library
ISBN 9781785032479

Design by Clarkevanmeurs Design Limited

Penguin Random House is committed to a sustainable future for
our business, our readers and our planet. This book is made from
Forest Stewardship Council® certified paper.

MIX
Paper from
responsible sources
FSC® C018179

Printed and bound in Great Britain by Clays Ltd, St Ives plc

Man
Points

THE DEFINITIVE GUIDE TO
MEASURING YOUR MANLINESS

EBURY
PRESS

CONTENTS

THE MEANING OF MANLINESS

Once upon a time, fixing an engine, doing woodwork or lighting a fire were skills every man had. When men gave up doing a lot of this stuff, they called it progress. Too late they realised they had abandoned things that they actually liked doing, things that made them feel like proper men in the first place.

In some ways it is much easier being a man these days, but in other ways it is so much harder. Most of us don't have to go down the pit, toil in the fields or fight in the trenches so much any more. This is, generally, a win. But on the flip side modern man is running a gauntlet: our masculinity is under attack from grooming products, cushy city life, and reduced opportunities to show off our manly prowess.

In our grandfathers' and fathers' day there were clear codes of behaviour and everyone knew what was expected: a firm handshake kept you on the right side of the line; hugging another man put you way over it. Nowadays, even rugby league players hug. And cry. It's a complex and confusing world.

Luckily help is at hand, and that's where *Man Points* comes in. Finally, a handy yardstick against which you can measure your manliness. A rule book, if you will, to clarify the laws of the game we call 'manhood' once and for all. In here you will find not just a list of activities designed to put you on the path to a more manly you, but the exact designation of just how many man points are available for each task. Discover the core skills that any chap should have in his toolbox of manly competence and see your man points total rise like the pointer on a 'test your strength' machine.

Some skills earn more man points than others; sometimes the less obvious ones can score more highly, reflecting the complex nature of modern manhood. You will find a scoresheet on page 176 where you can record your man-chievements, and chart your progress on the road to becoming a true alpha male, admired by men and desired by women.

However, as already noted, the world today is full of challenges and threats. It is vital to be alert, defending your man points and avoiding a backslide into being a soft-handed incompetent who can't read a map or take a punch. Turn to page 180 to make sure you're not letting yourself down.

Don't let the modern world challenge your manhood – with the help of *Man Points* you'll soon be as manly as parking a monster truck in a very tight space.

So eat the steak, grab your hammer and man up!

MAN POINTS

LIGHTING A FIRE WITHOUT MATCHES

Fire! The ability to create fire is what sets man apart from the animals. Real men command fire: it is their servant. Conjuring fire using just your wits and what nature provides is a major sign of manliness. When society collapses (or the heating breaks down) this skill will see you through the dark and dangerous night.

➤ You will need kindling. Hair makes good kindling to start a fire. In order of preference it goes: pubic, chest, head. Who knew pubes were so flammable? Finding kindling will be more difficult if you have been aggressively manscaping

➤ Once you have started your fire, you must tend it like a weak kitten: feed it small amounts, blow on it gently and shelter it from wind and rain

➤ Your goal is to eventually build a huge, roaring beast, around whose flickering flames you can dance naked in the night. Be warned, though, that some campsites frown on this kind of thing

NOTE: creating fire by setting light to your fringe using your girlfriend's hair straighteners does not count

UNBLOCKING A DRAIN

Unblocking a drain is one of those tasks historically allocated to men, despite statistics showing that women and children are responsible for 95% of all blocked drains. Think toys, hair and congealed hair products. But men who suggest that those who caused the problem should be the ones to fix it will find no one listening. It is your job, and no one else's, so strap on the rubber gloves and take up your plunger.

- Some drains are a tricky shape, and narrow. You might think that a small child's arm is perfect for reaching round a U-bend. Think again: having to phone the fire brigade to free a trapped infant from the toilet bowl is not an easy call to make

- Tools unblock stools. Many household items can be utilised to prod around: an umbrella, a poker, a wooden spoon. Be aware that some people might subsequently regard these items as no longer fit for their original purpose. Especially the spoon

- If you have to put your hand down into the murky unknown, be prepared. The worst-case scenario is touching something alive. Your instinct will be to scream and recoil, but stand firm. Instead, grasp the beast and hold it aloft for all to see how manly you are

SWIMMING OUTDOORS IN THE WINTER

A man should always take the opportunity to have an outdoor dip. However, if another man suggests it first then it is absolutely vital to join in or risk looking like a sissy.

➤ Do not worry about lack of kit. Pants or boxers are fine. Nudity is only really required on stag dos or those European beaches where it is local custom

➤ Go in properly. Getting wet to the belly button isn't a swim – you need to get your head and shoulders under. Dry hair is the mark of a coward

➤ Make sure you get a selfie. Ideally this should be you, wet in your pants, standing next to a fully clothed person shivering in their winter coat, on a godforsaken beach with the sun going down at 4pm

BREAKING DOWN A DOOR

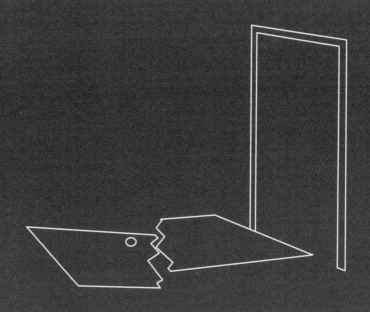

Breaking down a door isn't just for the drug squad, as any dad in possession of a small child and a too low bathroom door lock can tell you. The need to break a door down usually arises under dramatic circumstances, so it's crucial that you have a good technique. No one wants to see a man hopping round, toes broken but door still shut tight. Allocate a door in your house to practice on when everyone goes out.

- It's always best to break down a door with your boot. Shoulder charging can be effective, but be aware of inadvertent comedy mishaps should the door fling open

- Door breaking while intoxicated is extremely difficult due to coordination issues, even though being drunk and keyless is an all too common scenario. Don't be tempted to try. Either return to the pub or sleep it off in a bush

- It might take more than one kick. That's OK. Some doors are pretty solid. A general rule of thumb is: anything over five attempts is failure. Worst-case scenario? People start looking round for a real man to do it

GUTTING
AN ANIMAL

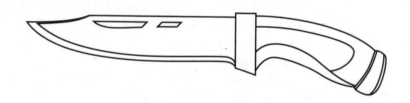

Disembowelling a dead animal is a tough task, and one that really separates the men from the vegetarians. Luckily there are numerous visceral internet videos presented by good ol' boys called things like Billy Bob Cooter, who delight in graphically showing you how to flay and gut a skunk to an invigorating banjo soundtrack.

➤ First things first. Make sure that the animal is dead

➤ Tools are important. You need a sharp knife. That's it. If you forget your knife then you're going to have to open that baby up with your bare teeth. That's worth a ton of man points, but the only person who will ever want to kiss those lips again is a survivalist called Dave

➤ When it comes to it, it's actually pretty easy. You just make a long hole in the undercarriage area and out should tumble all the tubes and pipes, which you then cut away. Don't start a tug of war with the guts: this will not end well, and you will never look at a sausage in the same way again

BUILDING FLAT-PACK FURNITURE

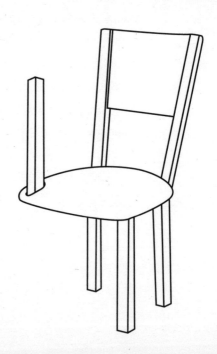

For many men, flat-pack furniture is kryptonite, rendering them weak and useless. The dangers lurking in seemingly innocent flat-pack kits are many. What if you're not strong enough to lift it into the car? What if you don't have the right tools? And worst of all, what if you can't do it and have to look on while your girlfriend finishes the job? The hints below will help you achieve a manly finish to your flat-pack, every time.

- Firstly, discard all instructions immediately. You do not need those

- Utilise your full range of tools, remembering to add the special tool that comes with the kit to your toolbox afterwards. Even though you will never remember what it is or where it came from

- The estimated time it should take to build is on the box. This is a direct challenge. You must beat this time, otherwise you will feel a failure every time you open the cupboard that took you three days to build

- Of course it doesn't fit together properly. That's because the legs were made in Sweden and the top in Papua New Guinea. This is not your fault. You have done a great job

READING
A MAP

Find your way everywhere by satnav or phone? Stop it. Using a good old fashioned map marks you out as a gritty outdoorsman, who goes to places satnav doesn't even know about. The only thing better than going by map is navigating by the sun and stars, but that can be tough unless you happen to own a sextant.

➤ First, check the map is the right way up. A handy way to tell is to check that the writing isn't upside down

➤ Maintain map control at all times. You are the navigator: an esteemed and noble role. Don't allow naysayers from the back seat to usurp your authority with claims that their phone is saying you are somewhere completely different

➤ Is your map accurate? Check. If it has a blank area with 'Here Be Dragons' written on it, then it may be time to update

20
POINTS

CARVING
MEAT

Carving meat not only gives you a chance to flaunt your superb knife skills, but your alpha status, too. When the roasted beast is brought to the table, you are the focus of attention. All the other diners unconsciously defer to you as the pack leader, which explains why who gets to carve the turkey often turns into a grim Christmas Day power struggle.

➤ Only offer to carve if the animal is sufficiently large and worthy of you. There is no glory in hacking at a microscopic quail, for example

➤ Meat is a pleasingly old-fashioned currency. Like a medieval king, you may confer favour on those who please you in the form of extra helpings of flesh

➤ Enjoy the opportunity to wheel out the classic 'are you a breast or leg man?' when serving other men. Unless it's your dad. Or your son

POINTS

CONQUERING A MOUNTAIN

When asked why he wanted to climb Everest, George Mallory answered, 'Because it's there.' Getting to the top of any peak is a thrill all men share, knowing they have conquered a mighty opponent. Even the sense of well-being you get looking down from the top escalator at the shopping centre isn't to be sniffed at.

- The more strenuous the ascent, the more points it accrues. Climbing or cycling up is worth maximum points. Arriving by cable car or tourist bus scores more lowly

- Dress appropriately. Do not be the idiot on the evening news being helicoptered off a fell wearing flip-flops and a sarong

- But do not be over-dramatic. You probably don't need crampons and an ice pick if there is a tea room full of old ladies at the summit

50 POINTS

DRINKING YOURSELF SOBER

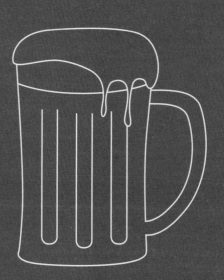

Drinking yourself back sober hardly ever occurs, but when it does it's never forgotten. This is a magical moment of alchemy and not something you can set out to do. For many men, this is as near as they'll ever get to achieving higher consciousness: an almost zen-like state.

➤ You can only drink yourself sober on certain drinks. Beer, yes. Tequlia, no

➤ Don't accuse the barman of diluting your drinks. Be proud. Pat yourself on the back, preferably just above the kidneys. They've done a great job

➤ Although you feel sober, obviously don't go to work, drive a car or make a marriage proposal. It might be that you are still very, very drunk

PUTTING UP A SHELF

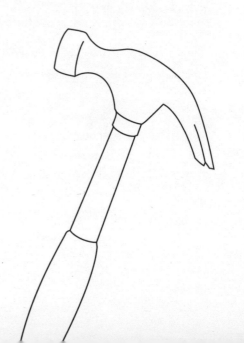

Rightly known as a classic test of manliness, in the father-in-law manual that is given to every male when a daughter reaches 18, 'Can he put up a shelf?' is in the top three key questions for a potential suitor. Shelf-hanging (always good to demonstrate knowledge by using the proper term) requires the essential core tools: drill, screwdrivers, level and, of course, the hammer. Any man who can competently command these can hold his head high.

➤ A shelf is a must in any man's abode to display the awards and statues that your sporting and social prowess have brought you. If you don't have any then a shelf is still handy. It's somewhere to put your anti-depressants

➤ Be creative. A shelf does not have to come from a shop. It can be a bit of wood from a skip balanced on some bricks. That's a shelf!

➤ It is manly to overload your shelf. Do not be tempted to display a few well-chosen pieces, thoughtfully arranged. Pile your shelf high. A base layer of books can be topped with DVDs, bottles of booze and even the odd sock or shoe. This also shows off how sturdy your shelf is

20
POINTS

EMPTYING A
MOUSETRAP

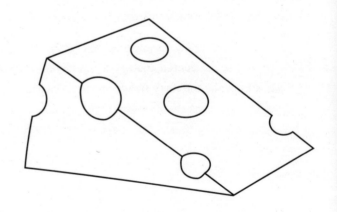

A no-win situation. Like drain unblocking [see p14], mousetrap emptying is a job men are expected to do. So refusing to do it is highly damaging, diminishing you in the eyes of others. Be warned though: showing relish is even worse. Would you want to hang out with someone who looked forward to disposing of dead vermin?

➤ A dead mouse is better than a live one. Mousetrap emptying can soon segue into a grisly killing nightmare. Got a cat? Send it in as an advance party to dispatch the wounded

➤ Like fishing, you might just get a big one. Have a camera and something you can lay alongside the carcass to indicate its relative size

➤ At the end of the day, it's just a dead mouse. Don't over-dramatise it and develop a haunted, thousand-yard stare. You went into the cupboard under the stairs, not on a tour of duty

20
POINTS

WIRING
A PLUG

Wiring a plug might seem mundane, but consider this: when you dabble with electricity you are taking on one of the most formidable powers in the known universe, one that can destroy buildings, melt steel, and bring death in an instant. That's why it matters that you know where the brown wire goes.

- As reading instructions or guides is not manly, memorise this simple sentence to help you remember where each wire goes: blue goes left, brown goes right and striped goes to the top. This applies to UK plugs

- In matters of wiring, being a bit UKIP is fine. Frankly, foreign plugs are a mess: different shaped holes, only two pins, incomprehensible symbols. Avoid interfering with these

- It is your honour to be the first to operate any device after giving it a new plug. This is known as the death or glory test, for obvious reasons. Invest in some rubber wellies, in case it goes a bit wrong

20 POINTS

EATING VERY SPICY FOOD

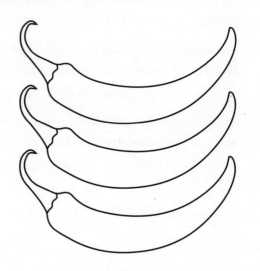

For a dank island where it is impossible to grow a proper chilli, the British love spicy food. Like whisky and beer, it is an acquired taste that takes work. Make sure you are not the weakling in the curry house who can only manage a mild dish.

- The hotter the spicing, the more manly it is. That's why everyone admires the daredevils who go off-menu in a curry house for the one served in an asbestos bowl

- To eat spicy food is to take part in a brave and manly tradition: think British army officers in full woollen military dress, eating fiery curry under the heat of the Indian sun

- After spicy food, be sensible. It's probably best not to arrange any activities for the next day that involve wearing white trousers. Or being too far from a toilet

50 POINTS

APPREHENDING A CRIMINAL

Go ahead, punk. Make my day. Who doesn't want to be a hero? Returning snatched handbags to grateful old ladies, or facing down street gangs with your unflinching glare. Successfully apprehending a criminal is potentially very dangerous and therefore very manly. Just make sure that they have committed a proper crime. Ringing the police because Keith next door parked over your drive again does not make you Dirty Harry.

- A crime has been committed! Adrenaline is pumping! But wait a second. Any sensible vigilante will take a few moments to assess the situation. What is the nature of the crime? Is it a bag snatch? Probably OK to intervene. A kidnap? Tricky, but rescuing a child comes with a huge hero bonus. Gunshots? What are you, a sheriff in the Wild West? Leave this one to the pros

- If you actually catch the felon and discover that he is so keen to remain at liberty that he has produced a weapon, you may back off, honour intact. After all, you have made an effort

- In extreme situations, learn from the films. Acts of fearless athleticism are the key here. If you manage this then you have publicly displayed your manliness. It doesn't actually matter if you apprehend the criminal or not

30 POINTS

TAKING A PUNCH

When it comes to punching, many hold to the traditional view that it is better to give than receive. There's a lot to be said in favour of this, not least by dentists, but being able to take a punch is a skill worth having. The key is to anticipate the hit, be prepared to take the pain, try not to go down, and definitely no crying.

- Most punches are aimed at the head. This is good news, as your head is pretty hard. If someone injures themselves punching you, add five bonus points

- Low blows don't count. If someone gets you below the belt, then the Rules of Combat allow you to drop to the floor without loss of manliness. Your assailant will lose man points for aiming at your swingers, and may well receive admonishment from any onlookers

- The reaction to aim for is an impassive stare, implying you didn't feel anything at all. This is when a man finds out what he is made of. If you find this is an implacable core of granite and steel, good for you. But if you find you are made of a mixture of snot, tears and a spreading warm trickle down your trousers, then you may as well just run away

POINTS

CHECKING OUT NOISES AT NIGHT

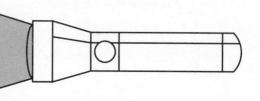

It is late at night, and dark outside. All is quiet. Suddenly, you hear a strange noise. It's coming from somewhere in your house! Is it a burglar? A stray cat? An unquiet spirit? A hockey-masked psycho? This is no time to quiver under the covers. Man up, get a grip and prepare to face the unknown.

- However scared you may be, it is never acceptable to make your wife or girlfriend go and see what it is making the noise

- Make maximum noise as you go. Convey to any intruder the impression that a 20-stone lump of angry muscle is thumping down the stairs towards them

- On returning, make a full report to your bedmate to emphasise your courage. If they are asleep, wake them to tell them that they can now rest easy

PLAYING
SPORT WITH A
HANGOVER

Playing sport with a hangover is a rite of passage. While performance may be down as you see two balls at once and the white lines on the pitch seem to be moving about, your suffering provides an excellent bonding exercise as your teammates laugh at you throwing up on the side of the pitch and collapsing into a muddy puddle.

- Teammates will rally round to dispense sage medical advice. Unfortunately for you, this is always the time-honoured 'sweat it out' cure, so get on with it

- As crap as you feel, remember that someone else has had it worse than you. There is always a club legend about someone called Big Steve who was sick on the referee before falling asleep on the penalty spot

- However bad your hangover, after the match you must go to the pub with your teammates and start drinking. Sloping off home/ordering a soft drink is not permitted under current UK amateur sports laws

SAILING A WATERBORNE CRAFT

Commanding any kind of vessel upon open water is worth man points. There is a sliding scale, with fewest points awarded to captaining a pedalo, while maximum is scored by helming an aircraft carrier (110 to be exact). The sea (or boating lake) can be a cruel mistress, and any man who ventures forth deserves respect.

- Learn some nautical phrases. Talking about sheets, jibs and gunwales will help you fit right in with the sailing set

- Singing sea shanties is great when out at sea, on a creaking deck with sails cracking overhead. In a rowing boat on the park pond? Probably not

- However tempted by the romance of it all NEVER BUY A BOAT. You'll get more happiness and satisfaction flushing £20 notes down the toilet. Not for nothing do they say that the two happiest days of a sailor's life are the day he buys a boat and the day he sells it

30 POINTS

BREWING YOUR OWN BEER

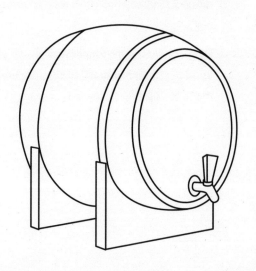

Brewing your own beer sits at the sweet spot of science and self-sufficiency. It's an ancient art, too: men have been drinking fermented liquor since they wanted to let off steam at the end of a hard week slaying mastodons.

- The power of your beer is directly proportional to manliness: aim for something that is roughly the strength of wine

- Now you are a brewer, take the opportunity to set up a small pub or bar area in your house. Friends will enjoy coming round to sample your every batch

- Remember to add a veneer of sophistication to your finished product by adding the word 'craft' to your brew e.g. Dave's Craft Garage-matured Lager

POINTS

PARKING

So integral is the ability to park to manliness that some men have preferred to drive on and walk back five miles, rather than face the pressure of having to squeeze into a tight parking space. Is there any more humiliating sight than that of a grown man in his car taking instructions from someone on the pavement on how to get into a tight spot?

- If your car has parking sensors, turn them off. They were not fitted for you

- However much trouble it gets you into, it is part of your DNA as a man to dispense advice and instruction to any female you see parking their car. You must accept this and they may too

- For maximum man points, try Ultimate Parking: approach your intended space as fast as you can, before slamming on the brakes to skid perfectly into place

POINTS

DRINKING
ALL NIGHT

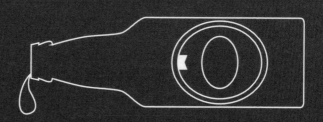

Being in the pub when the landlord pulls back the curtains to let in the early morning sunlight is one of those special moments in any man's life. Being able to last the night through, though, doesn't happen by accident. It takes dedication and skill: remember, it's a marathon, not a sprint.

- Start slow. Chugging back four pints of lager in the first hour is an amateur mistake

- Food is essential, but only snacks. Limit yourself to traditional carb-based snacks sold behind the bar. If the options stretch to artisan olives and quail's eggs then you are in the wrong bar

- Stay social. He who slumps into silence in the corner isn't going to make it. Keep chatting: no one's going to remember what you said, anyway

35 POINTS

ORDERING DINNER FOR SOMEONE ELSE

A controversial entry, fraught with risk. Ordering dinner for someone else is a powerful indicator of confidence and worldliness. Think James Bond: here is a man who knows what he wants, and what a woman wants too. But can a modern man ever get away with this, or did ordering for the lady go out when Sean Connery still had hair?

➤ If you order for your dinner companion, project certainty, confidence and (if possible) charm. Whatever you do, don't hesitate over the choices. Dithering will not inspire confidence in your dinner companion*

➤ Pick your restaurant sensibly. Telling the teen at the counter that the lady will have cheese and beans on her potato does not make you a suave playboy

➤ Of course, there is one further category. This is the mandatory requirement that you order dinner for any friend on his stag night. Here, convention dictates that you must order the hottest, spiciest and most painful meal possible, then sit back and insist that he finishes all of it

* TOP TIP: ladies seldom eat offal. The last recorded instance was when the Queen Mother ate a devilled kidney for breakfast at Balmoral in 1985

50 POINTS

BUILDING A SHED

Shed building is a noble art; essentially the construction of a whole building. This puts man in direct contact with his forebears: the pharaohs who built the pyramids; the Romans and their coliseums; kings and their mighty castles. All look down through history and nod approvingly at the shed-builder.

- A shed is an erection for the ages. It is therefore advisable to get out every tool you own, plus exhibit much use of string and spirit levels. Shut one eye and peer at a raised right thumb at intervals

- The key tool is a hammer. A shed cannot be over-hammered, and it is an ideal way to let your neighbours hear that you are doing something manly

- Aim for walls that are perpendicular to the floor, which should mostly be covered by the roof

TOP TIP: on no account may you paint the exterior of your shed. Did the pioneers paint their log cabins in Burnt Aubergine by Farrow & Ball? No

5

POINTS

EATING MEAT

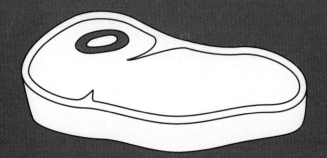

It might sound obvious but eating meat is essential for manliness. Red meat is the most manly: steak is king. If you know nothing else about cookery, you should know one thing: how you like your steak.

- Red meat should, ideally, bleed on your plate a bit. When the waiter asks you how you want it cooked, 'well done' is not an acceptable answer. You might as well ask mummy to cut it up for you, too

- Always eat meat with your hands, if you can. Gnawing on ribs or the wing of a chicken is the natural order of things: cutlery is an affectation of the feckless and weak

- If you must eat fish, make sure it's a manly one like shark. That you have caught yourself, ideally by using dynamite or a harpoon

GETTING A TABLE IN A BOOKED-OUT RESTAURANT

Getting a table at a fancy restaurant when you haven't booked is advanced man points stuff. It takes a mixture of nerve, charm, persistence and quick wits to break through the formidable defences of the maître d'. Restaurants always have a table for the right walk-in customer. That customer is you.

➤ Be confident. Starting with 'I don't suppose you have a table for two...' will guarantee failure. You must expect to get a table. YOUR table

➤ Lay it on thick. Gesture to your girlfriend and whisper that it is a special occasion. Be careful, though. You might end up having to propose just to keep the lie alive

➤ Spread the wealth. If you get a table, a discrete tip is in order. This should be a note, slipped into the palm. Do not count out 20p pieces into the maître d's hand

DRINKING NEAT WHISKY

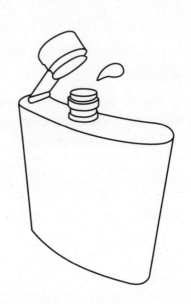

If alcopops are the nursery slopes of booze, then neat whisky is the black run to which all men aspire. Whisky is a serious drink, drunk by real men. Did Winston Churchill plan D-Day with a strawberry daiquiri in his hand? No, he did not.

- Be realistic. No one likes their first taste of whisky. Remember, though, that if you are in company you must suppress your inner toddler and hide your distaste

- Adopt a whisky lifestyle. When you get home from work, throw your coat on a chair and pour yourself a couple of fingers while instructing your life partner how you'd like your steak cooked. Good luck

- Develop a taste for a particular single malt. The rarer and more expensive the better, to reflect your experienced and refined palate

POINTS

HITCH-HIKING

The man who hitch-hikes is an adventurer who feels the romance of the open road, and who has a wild, untamed spirit. He may also be a man who can't afford his train fare, but let us not dwell on that. Every man should try hitch-hiking at least once. When he does he steps outside the boundaries of the conventional and into the unknown (or, if he's unlucky, into the passenger seat of a Peugeot bound for Swindon). Hit the road!

- Dress appropriately. Too scruffy, and potential lifts will ignore you as a tramp. Slicked-back hair, a three piece suit and briefcase standing on the verge of the road marks you out as a potential psycho, though. Aim for somewhere in between

- A sign showing your destination can be a great help. Don't be over-specific though. Something like 'the West' is usefully broad. '32 Laburnam Drive, WE12' is probably a bit optimistic

- Hitch-hike with a lady – this increases your chance of being picked up. Unfairly, perhaps, people see a couple as less threatening. Have they never seen *Bonnie and Clyde*?

BUILDING
A RAFT

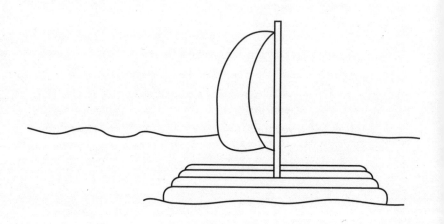

This is probably not a skill that you'll need often, but every man should know how to lash together a raft, just in case. You might, one day, end up stranded on an island. We've all seen *Lost*. And if warnings about global warming are true, then you might soon need one just to get to the corner shop.

- How big do you want your raft? Big enough for just you? Or do you want to take your most treasured possessions? Make room for your flat-screen TV and George Foreman grill

- As a modern man, you're not limited to traditional logs for your raft. Empty beer barrels are perfect. And if they are not empty – you know what to do!

- Take a repelling weapon. In desperate times other, less manly men might try to board your raft. You need to beat those scurvy dogs back!

30
POINTS

BUYING DIY
STUFF

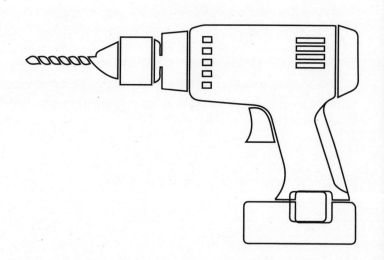

All men live in fear when it comes to visiting the hardware shop. Who wants to be the fool asking for 'the tap thingy'? There is nothing more intimidating than a small shop, with a cluster of tradesmen at the counter who stop their banter when you enter in anticipation of your humiliation. Follow these hints, and you'll be able to come across as a proper handyman.

- Dress appropriately. This means old, battered clothes. For obvious reasons do not rock up wearing white jeans and espadrilles

- If you've got a broken thing you need to replace, then take it with you. Slap it down on the counter and ask for a new one, cleverly avoiding having to describe it

- Massive bonus points if you know the name of something and the bloke serving doesn't. The internet is your friend here, helping you learn the names of all sorts of obscure gaskets and flanges

HUGGING (DONE RIGHT)

The manliness of hugging is a thorny issue and needs to be addressed here. Do not feel obliged to hug. Our forefathers did not. Consider the Victorians: the British Empire covered half the world, yet nowhere in it did two Englishmen embrace. But we live in complex times, which has embraced embracing. These tips will help you navigate a touchy-feely world.

- A brief, manly hug is fine. But don't accessorise your hug with kissing on cheeks, unless you are being made in the Mafia

- Beware when meeting an American, the stormtroopers of the hugging world. Their shock and awe weapon is the bear hug, and they deploy it without mercy. Especially in California

- Group hugs are just weird. Stay away, you have no place here

POINTS

RIDING A
MOTORBIKE

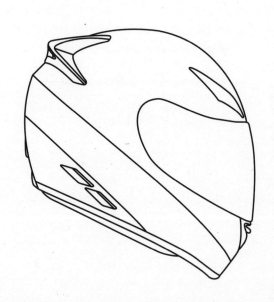

What man doesn't want the thrill of a powerful machine between his legs? Mastering the steel horse takes nerve and guts. Interestingly, it is also one of the few opportunities to legitimately wear leather trousers.

- Disabuse yourself of the idea that you can ride a motorbike because you once hired a moped on holiday on a Greek island. If you rode it wearing flip-flops, that wasn't a motorbike

- A motorcycle is inherently cool. Think Steve McQueen. Don't ruin it by attaching streamers to the handlebars, or a novelty horn

- Not for nothing is the motorbike known to medics as the Donorcycle. Once you've learned to ride one, that's enough. Pocket the points and step away from the bike

POINTS

TRAVELLING LIGHT

Real men pack light. Scientists have even developed an equation that finds the precise packing needed for any holiday, which is number of pants = number of days divided by two. For the non-scientific, follow this rule of thumb: a week's packing should fit in a carrier bag with enough room left to fit in one bottle of duty free.

➢ If you must take luggage, the golden rule is nothing wheeled. Do you want people to think you can't manage to lift a case?

➢ Improvise. Tuck a toothbrush behind your ear. Let your swimming trunks double as pants. Wear your wetsuit onto the aircraft

➢ Don't forget to display your lean, mean packing skills to the rest of your flight. Make eye contact with every poor sucker stuck at baggage claim while you stride on through, swinging your solitary carrier bag

40 POINTS

CHOPPING WOOD

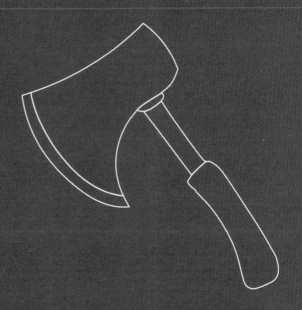

Chopping up wood with an axe is shorthand for manliness. This is a quintessential activity of men through the ages to keep the home fires burning through the bitter winter, while wolves and bears roam the bleak wilderness outside. It doesn't matter if you live in a terraced house in Slough. You are man. You are chopping wood. **ROAR!**

➤ Wood must be chopped, not sawn. So get an axe. A big one

➤ Once you've finished your hard day's chopping, you can sit by your fire and lovingly sharpen your mighty axe, just like old woodsmen used to

➤ Chopping wood can be hot work. If there are ladies around it may be beneficial to remove your shirt. *Little House on the Prairie* hunk-of-the-month is the look you are aiming for

SHOPPING FOR CLOTHES (DONE RIGHT)

Shopping for clothes is tricky because it carries the risk of being mistaken for someone who cares what they look like. But unless he is to go naked, man must have clothes. Many men subcontract this activity to mothers, girlfriends and wives. The latter two are permissible, but anyone over 16 whose mum is still buying their clothes needs urgent counselling. Do not despair: shopping can, under some circumstances, score man points.

- Shopping for clothes for dangerous activities is OK. Buying a Kevlar vest before departing to a war zone is good, masculine shopping

- Only shop when your existing wardrobe has become an affront to civilised society. Browsing is not allowed. Simply march into the first shop, select the required item, pay and leave. Real men don't know where the changing rooms are

- Visiting a tailor is OK. If he fitted your father and his father before him, all the better. This is not shopping: this is the upholding of a proud male tradition

10 POINTS

WET SHAVING

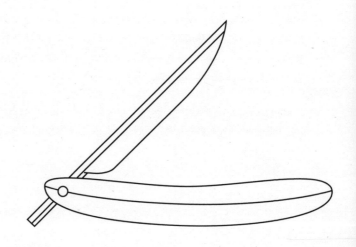

Shaving is a rite of passage, marked by ritual bloodletting: teenage boys keen to begin shaving, hacking at their bum-fluff with their mum's leg razor. When the beard starts to grow in earnest, the only proper way to shave is to wet shave. If you need a manly image to aim for, think of a soldier in the trenches shaving in the reflection of his hip flask before going over the top.

> Wet shaving is the acceptable face of male grooming. This is your 'me' time in the bathroom, so lock the door and work up that lather. No scented candles, though

> Never be tempted to go for an electric shaver. They reek of desperation, of angry photocopier salesman shaving in their rear-view mirror in a motorway services car park

> Your shaving kit should be treated with respect. Hide it away, lest your partner decides to use it to shave her legs

POINTS

HAVING A SCAR

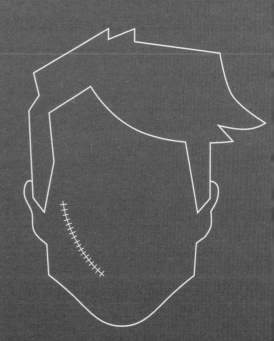

As all young boys learnt from Action Man, having a scar is proof of toughness. Any man worth his salt should have at least one scar, preferably somewhere that is easily noticed. A scar shouldn't be too ostentatious. Ideally it should be like an expensive watch: discrete, tasteful and preferably obtained on an adventure to the Swiss Alps.

➤ One must never show scars off uninvited. Only when noticed is it permissible to reveal it for further inspection. Scars below the waist should only be viewed by appointment

➤ Scars from operations do not count, unless that operation was to repair damage sustained while doing something manly. For example, the scar from being stitched up having fended off a wolverine attack is OK. The scar from having a gastric band fitted isn't

➤ There is a cut-off point. If you find you have more scars than you have had birthdays then it's time to re-evaluate. Maybe it's time to retire from drinking?

20
POINTS

WHITTLING

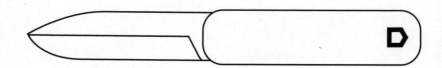

Whittling is an under-appreciated pastime definitely due for a comeback. Carving a lump of wood round the fire was how our forefathers relaxed before the invention of the box set. Whittling is made more manly by choosing to fashion either a weapon of some kind, or a lewd sculpture. It also gives you a legitimate excuse to browse great big knives that normally you have no business even looking at.

- Traditionally, whittling is done in a rocking chair, on a porch, in the bayou. But really you can whittle anywhere in the home, including on the toilet

- However, it is probably best not to pull out your knife to do some whittling on the bus or train home from work

- Try whittling something to present as a gift to someone you admire. Hint: ladies might appreciate a delicately carved small bird more than a wooden replica of the FA Cup

FIRING A GUN

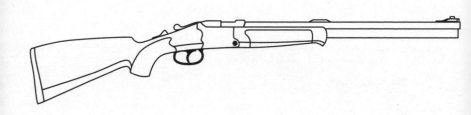

Firing a gun makes you more manly. Fact. But only in the eyes of other men. Women, oddly, generally look at men and guns with pitying scorn, dismissing it as barely repressed willy waving. Men, though, know that gathering together (often in the woods), and excitedly playing with things that shoot off in your hand is very manly indeed.

➤ Finding a gun to shoot can be difficult. You will need to befriend people at the borders of society, who tend to be more likely to be gun owners. At one extreme, the posh boy from work called Jolyon whose father is a Lord; at the other, the feral youth outside the all-night garage. Choose wisely

➤ Shooting at something is even more manly; boosted further if you manage to hit your target. You might even get to eat what you have shot, providing extra man point opportunities (see gutting an animal, p20 and lighting a fire p12)

➤ Firing a gun, like making a bomb joke to airport security, is something to be done with extreme caution. If in doubt, consider the anecdote that will result from your actions. Shooting off a TV aerial by mistake? That's funny. Literally shooting yourself in the foot? No

15 POINTS

TYING A
BOW TIE

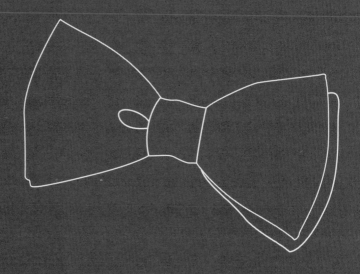

Tying a bow tie is a skill all men should have, because without it you can't achieve the classic look of an untied one. Standing outside the casino in Monte Carlo at dawn, the man with the untied bow tie is the debonair risk-taker who put it all on black and lost. But he doesn't care; he's still got the keys to his Ferrari. But who's that in the background, with what looks like a dead blackbird stuck to his shirt? Only some loser with a clip-on dicky bow at half mast.

- Tying a bow tie isn't that hard. If you can do up your shoe laces, you can tie one. If you're still relying on Velcro to fasten your shoes, then you're probably not really ready for a bow tie

- Being able to tie a bow tie isn't an excuse to wear one willy-nilly. Bow ties should be black, and worn at night, ideally in some sort of James Bond setting. Coloured, flashing or spinning ones are strictly forbidden

- Never start the evening with the tie undone. This is dishonest. An untied bow tie is a badge of honour that signifies that a night of serious partying has taken place. You have to earn the right

EATING OLD FOOD

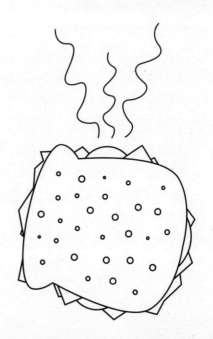

Eating out of date food can sometimes be a matter of survival: what better cure for a hangover than some of that old chicken tikka that's been in the back of the fridge since Tuesday? But it can also be a matter of principal and pride. Best Before and Use By dates are for weaklings who don't enjoy your iron constitution.

➤ Always carry out a visual inspection of the food first. Green fur can be scraped off. But if it is moving or has developed its own fledgling ecosystem it may have ceased to be food

➤ Chilli sauce will usually improve anything that, frankly, tastes a bit weird

➤ And remember, you are not too cheap to throw food away, you are staging a protest against consumerism and waste

30

POINTS

DIAGNOSING ENGINE TROUBLE

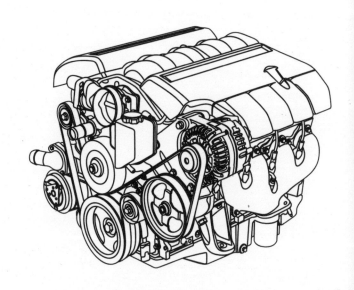

Never forgo the chance to offer advice to the stricken motorist. Don't let your lack of knowledge about mechanical matters stand in the way. Just remember to be on your way before anyone who actually knows what they are talking about turns up.

- Never overlook the obvious. If you see a cat or nest of birds under the bonnet, chances are that that's the problem. Livestock has no place in modern engines

- The phrase 'the big end's gone' is often the most useful in this scenario. Rest assured that no one really knows what this means

- Offering to push a broken-down car gives a chance to demonstrate your strength and physique. Minus points if straining to push causes stress incontinence

DEMOLISHING SOMETHING

The yin to the yang of building a shed, demolishing stuff is just as important. What man doesn't thrill at the sight of the wrecking ball? The tougher and bigger the thing you demolish, the more manly it is. The urge to knock things down is part of man's DNA, an anthropological fact demonstrated every time a small boy on a beach kicks over his sister's sandcastle.

➤ Demolition offers the chance to use some really serious tools. Sledgehammers, pneumatic drills and chainsaws all gladden the heart of a real man

➤ The most manly way to demolish anything is to punch it to the ground. Punching a shed apart is one of the highest-scoring man activities of all

➤ Go carefully. Once the full demolishing frenzy takes hold it is easy to rampage too far. For example, avoid smashing out of your own house and into your neighbour's

POINTS

NOT GOING
TO THE
DOCTOR

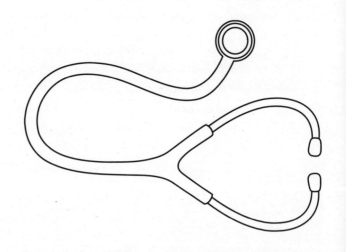

Most ailments usually sort themselves out, don't they? Besides, what can medics really do? They haven't even discovered a cure for the common cold yet. With a bit of practice you can become your own GP.

➤ Assemble your own version of the doctor's black bag. It should contain pliers (for pulling stuff out), superglue (for sticking cuts) and vodka (for sterilising and pain relief). That's it

➤ Avoid symptom checking on the internet. This only leads to paranoia and late-night visits to A&E claiming you have contracted a rare strain of bubonic plague. Don't be that guy

➤ Use your unhealthiest-looking friend as your benchmark. If even he says you look a bit rough, then it's probably time to book an appointment, just in case

45

POINTS

GETTING OUT
OF A SKID

A high scoring activity, skidding requires the manly combo of fast driving, lightning reflexes and audacious car control. Skids are always better if there's another man in the car: women, sadly, don't appreciate a good skid – a life lesson that is as valuable in the laundry room as it is the car.

➤ If your car goes into a skid, remember to turn the wheel in the same direction to get out of it. More importantly, keep an impassive demeanour. This is cool. The only movement should be in your hands as they expertly dance on the steering wheel

➤ Everyone skids their cars when it is icy and snowy. Therefore it is more manly to make a point of never skidding in slippery conditions

➤ Getting out of a skid by crashing your car into a tree does not count

30
POINTS

CARRYING HEAVY THINGS

Sometimes a man needs to display his raw power and might, unfiltered. This is why lifting and carrying things is so important. This isn't about being a muscle-bound gym-freak the size of a small car: skinny guys can lift heavy things too. Shopping bags, sofas, children: there are multiple opportunities to demonstrate your power in everyday life.

> The main thing is to carefully assess whether you can actually do it. Not much is more humiliating than firmly seizing a box of flat-pack furniture only to fail to raise it more than an inch before it crashes back down (see p22)

> Once off the ground, the key is to make what you're carrying seem not that heavy. So no gasping or grunting. You alone know that if someone else tried it the weight would literally crush them

> Don't confuse this with lifting weights in the gym. Lifting heavy furniture scores much better than pumping iron with a bunch of oiled narcissists while looking in the mirror

45
POINTS

REMAINING A
BACHELOR

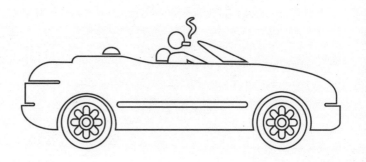

In the past, remaining a bachelor was considered extremely manly. People understood that the gent in question had cunningly managed to evade the world of marriage and domesticity to enjoy a full life of sports car driving, romantic picnics on riverbanks and firm-jawed pipe smoking. Nowadays, though, it is much more complicated. It is important to consider these points:

- Move out of the parental home. You cannot be the right kind of bachelor and live with your mum. Living in the loft does not count as moving out

- Your car needs only two seats, and a boot just big enough for a weekend bag or set of clubs. You will never carry more. The supermarket and DIY superstore are places unknown to you

- Be wary of social media. Would James Bond tweet, update his relationship status or post stuff on his blog?

40 POINTS

DEALING WITH AN ANGRY ANIMAL

Man is king of the beasts. Sometimes, though, you might just need to remind a critter just who is boss. Obviously, this is more straight forward with some animals than with others. An angry gerbil is tricky, but easier to deal with than an enraged pit bull.

➤ The best way to avoid dealing with angry animals is to minimise the risk of being around them. To this end, never go on safari, to the zoo or even visit a pet shop

➤ Should an animal start giving you an evil look and signalling it is about to attack, remain calm. Remember: it is easier to remain calm when up a tree or hiding in your car

➤ Experts recommend startling an animal to shock it out of its rage. In the case of dogs, shock tactics include sticking a finger up its rectum. You may prefer to just get bitten

GIVING A SPEECH

Giving a speech is a proper test of manliness, requiring courage and confidence. Don't confuse giving a speech with speaking at meetings: we're not talking about running through a PowerPoint on quarterly sales here. A speech is about your ability to hold and control an audience.

➤ Nerves are normal, but don't hit the booze too hard beforehand. As a minimum, you should be able to stand unaided

➤ Preparation is key. Know what you are going to say, but have a few options up your sleeve. Some of those salty anecdotes in the best man's speech might have to go when you notice the bride comes from a family of clergymen

➤ Avoid inside jokes. Unless you are speaking at a secret society, in which case it should be all inside jokes

60 POINTS

FLYING A PLANE

Probably not something that you'll be called upon to do much, but lots of man points are available if you can step up when the call goes out, 'Is there anyone on this flight who can fly a plane?' This is your moment. Act confident, follow these steps, and it should be plain sailing.

➤ First things first. Establish basic manoeuvres. Pushing the controls away from you sends the plane down. Pulling back brings it back up. Or vice versa. Why not experiment?

➤ Can you contact ground control? They'll be able to help you. Remember to throw in lots of 'Roger, Roger' type jargon to demonstrate your competence to the guys on the ground

➤ Should it transpire that no, actually, you cannot fly a plane after all, prepare your passengers for the inevitable by whistling 'Always Look on the Bright Side of Life' over the intercom. They'll soon get the hint

35
POINTS

SMOKING
A CIGAR

Whether you actually smoke is irrelevant; smoking cigars is what men do. And of all smoking, it's the one that gets a pass: no man ever got told off for having a cigar when wetting the baby's head, for example. But you don't just fire up and puff away. Here's how to do it properly:

- Good, proper cigars have a blunt end. This needs to be cut. Don't try to bite it off like Clint Eastwood. You'll just get a soggy, frayed end and brown bits of cigar in your teeth

- Use a long match to light it. A short one will burn your fingers before you've got it going properly

- But be prepared, this thing is going to take a while to smoke. Unless your boss is extremely forgiving, cigars are not suitable for your mid-morning fag break

ANTI-MAN POINTS

-25 POINTS

BEING IN TOUCH WITH YOUR FEELINGS

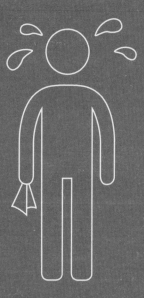

The average Englishman treats his emotions like a distant cousin. If he met them on a bus, he would nod politely, and go and sit three rows behind. This is the correct state of affairs. A real man:

- Was bemused by the outpouring when Princess Di died. What was wrong with people?

- Never carries a hanky to dab tears: only to staunch wounds

- Would rather talk about their parents' sex life than their feelings, but ideally would talk about nothing

-30

POINTS

DANCING WITH BOTH HANDS IN THE AIR

It is impossible to dance with your hands in the air and remain manly. Dancing is a difficult area for men and it's usually safest to stick to a few approved moves; for example, stepping from side to side, jumping up and down and air guitar. If in doubt, follow these guidelines:

> You may raise one hand occasionally to do an air punch if the song demands it. But one hand only, remember

> Ideally your arms should remain clamped to your sides. Think Irish dancing

> Other banned moves include dancing round an object like a bag and twerking. Never, ever shake your booty

-35 POINTS

HAVING A RUBBISH HANDSHAKE

Your handshake is like a physical CV. You're telling people what sort of person you are when you shake hands. Men shake on a deal – a handshake is your personal guarantee that you're a sound bloke.

> Don't be a limp fish. A weak, loose grip says that you are untrustworthy, devious and probably kick puppies when no one's looking

> But don't go in too hard. A vice-like crush marks you out as an insecure overcompensator, unable to tell between a greeting and strength test

> A straight down the line handshake is best. Complicated street-style fist bumps and clenches will make you look a twat in that business meeting

-50
POINTS

NOT KNOWING HOW TO RIDE A BIKE

Learning how to ride a bike is a landmark event in any boy's life. Independence, freedom, adventure: what man wouldn't want those? Plus it can provide one of the few legitimate opportunities to wear Lycra.

- It might not be something you have to ever use, but bike riding is a skill you should have in your locker, just in case

- Fear of crashing is no reason to not learn to ride a bike: in fact, crashing can be cool and very manly

- Riding a bike contains an element of danger. Dangerous activities equals man points

-40

POINTS

GOING ON A SLEEPOVER

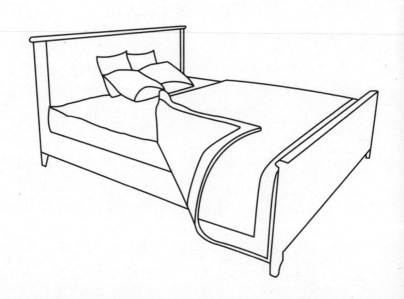

Most real men will never even have reason to use this word, but there are certain circumstances when it is OK for a man to stay overnight at his friend's place. These situations generally involve alcohol, peril or being in prison.

➤ Crashing at a mate's place isn't a sleepover. As the word 'crash' implies, this is more of an emergency landing situation

➤ Mass 'sleepovers' are OK if they follow something like a stag night. The higher the level of alcohol consumption in the day, the more legit they are

➤ Anything that involves white wine, Kettle Chips, wearing a onesie or a *Twilight* DVD immediately causes a catastrophic loss of man points

-20 POINTS

SHARING AN UMBRELLA

Some things that lose man points are daft. What's wrong with two men sharing an umbrella? Surely if it's a large enough umbrella it's sensible, and better than getting wet. And yet two men sharing an umbrella is somehow wrong. It's an irrefutable law of the universe.

➤ If it's a two men/one umbrella situation then etiquette dictates that the one with the umbrella should put it away, to avoid any awkwardness. Better to both get wet

➤ It is acceptable to stand under another man's umbrella if you are lighting a cigarette. Once lit, though, you must step back out

➤ Objects that men may shelter together under: trees, bus stops, pub awnings. Never: in doorways, under a shared coat, in a phone box

**-35
POINTS**

BEING SCARED
OF SPIDERS

Some people claim that being afraid of spiders and creepy-crawlies is a natural instinct we evolved to protect ourselves in the wild from poisonous bites and stings. These people are just excuse-mongering cowards: fear is only there to be conquered.

➤ There's a spider in the room. Where do you want to be? Up on a chair, screeching with the ladies? While you're up there, why not discuss your favourite episode of *Sex and the City*?

➤ Be bold. Don't bother with trying to trap it in a glass. Just pick it up. Try to enjoy the wriggling, tickling sensation in your palm, even if every fibre in your being is suppressing a scream

➤ Be kind. Release it back into the wild so another man gets the chance to demonstrate his bravery

-45
POINTS

READING
INSTRUCTIONS

Did the Romans include instructions with their giant catapults? No! Did English yeomen get a manual with their longbow? Of course not! They just got on with it, and worked it out for themselves. Trial and error is the only true path. Instructions are for wimps.

➤ So you follow instructions. Do you want to be a follower? Exactly!

➤ You get a much greater sense of achievement and well-being (and man points) if you manage to do something without having to look at the instructions

➤ Instructions are for risk-averse cowards. Improvisation and instinct are all you need. And a hammer, probably

-15

POINTS

OWNING MORE THAN THREE PAIRS OF SHOES

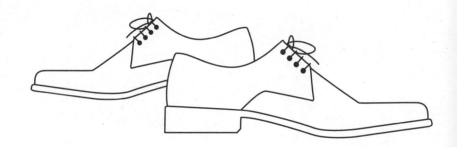

Why would any man need more than three pairs of shoes? After all, Alexander the Great famously only had one pair of sandals, and he conquered half the known world.

➤ One pair should be smart, for going to work/appearing in court. Another pair for sport. And a pair for everything else. That's it

➤ Buying shoes for a special occasion is not acceptable. There should be no event for which one of your three pairs will not be suitable

➤ As a real man, you will never own a pair of sandals

-30
POINTS

WEARING JORTS

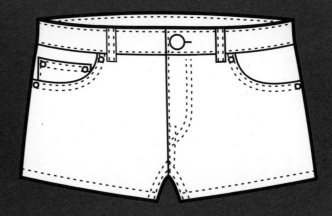

Jorts, for those who don't know, are jean shorts. Let's pause for a moment, and imagine your dad wearing jorts. You see! All man points gone in a flash. Go out wearing these and your reputation will be ashes.

- When your jeans are worn out, bin them. Don't be tempted to reach for the scissors to make them into jorts

- If you see another man wearing a pair, it is your duty to the brotherhood to immediately stage an intervention to help him

- If you find yourself wavering, remember: like skirts or high heels, jorts are best left to the ladies

SMELLING WRONG

A little manly musk is fine. But too much of the wrong kind of smell, and your points will disappear as fast as your friends.

- A slight tang of sweat, after sport for instance, is OK. But never let yourself go full tramp, and start to absolutely reek. Smelling like a load of men's old socks is unhygienic, not manly

- But don't over-perfume either. A man whose aftershave arrives in a room before he enters and leaves 10 minutes after he's gone is a laughing stock. Or an Italian

- Don't smell of the wrong thing. If you live with a woman the bathroom is likely to be riddled with all sorts of flowery smelling potions. Be on your guard and avoid these at all costs

-30 POINTS

GOING TO A
HAIRDRESSER

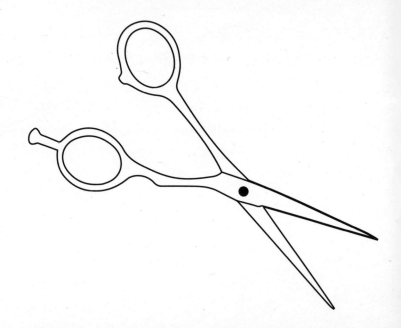

In North Korea there is a list of approved haircuts for men, which any barber can do. You go in, pick a number between 1 and 20, and 10 minutes later out you come, job done. There is something to be said for this approach. Going for a haircut should involve minimal time, conversation and eye contact.

➤ A barber is a hair cutting place for men. A hairdresser, salon or parlour is not. There can be no confusion

➤ Barbers do not offer hair dyeing, piercing or eyebrow shaping services. This is a good thing, as all lead to loss of man points

➤ Do not become one of those people who insist on having the same person cut your hair 'because they know how you like it'. When it comes to haircuts, you take what you're given

-INFINITE

POINTS

KNOWING THE CHARACTERS IN SEX AND THE CITY

Some men would protest that this might be accidental knowledge. 'Oh, it just slipped into my brain!' Knowing the name of one of the characters is unfortunate. Two and there is a pattern emerging. You must now sacrifice half of your man points. If you've seen the *Sex and the City* movie (even for 'research'), then you are a hopeless case and there's nothing to be done for you.

> This was a TV show about neurotic women, relationships and shoes (according to Wikipedia). What were you thinking?

> If the travails of single women looking for love in New York really struck a chord with you, then you must immediately go on a strict detox of martial arts films and beer

> All is not lost. You're not quite at rock bottom. That's for men who watched *Desperate Housewives*

-20 POINTS

DOING YOGA

People take up yoga to relax and find inner peace. An obvious waste of time, as peace and relaxation are easily found with a few pints, and without all that unnecessary bending. If you want to get fit, a few chin-ups each morning should be enough. No man needs yoga.

➤ Yoga is famous for its ability to induce flatulence. If you want to fart in public, save it for a night out with your mates who'll appreciate it properly

➤ A man who goes to yoga to meet girls is misguided. They might look good in Lycra, but their idea of a wild night is to sit around meditating in front of a candle

➤ Yoga makes you boring. Sorry, but there it is

BEING
SCARED
OF POWER
TOOLS

Men enjoy their tools. Even if they have no intention of buying, there are always men just browsing the tools aisle, admiring the drills and chainsaws. Yes, there is an inherent risk in using power tools, but that is what makes them manly.

➤ You must overcome your fear. Buy a drill and practise at home. Better a house riddled with holes than an unmanly phobia

➤ If you're scared of tools, think of the consequences. You'll have to get a man in to do your DIY. Why not ask him to take your girlfriend out for a good time while he's about it, too?

➤ If you fear power tools then you will never know the secret pleasures of the tool belt and the sanctuary of the home workshop

-40 POINTS

MANSCAPING

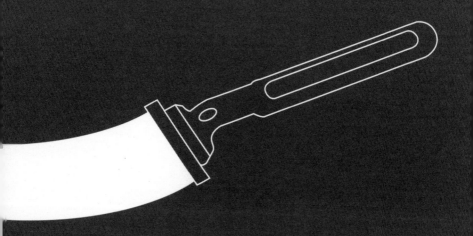

When men shave, wax or pluck out their body hair they are manscaping. While no one wants to look like a werewolf, the full fur look can easily be avoided by wearing a neck chain. Simply shave down to this line and you're good to go, preserving your man points.

➤ Remember. Shaving your beard is fine. Anything lower is not

➤ Manscapers are part of the metrosexual tribe. Metrosexuals are men who have never changed a tyre, put up a shelf or been in a fight

➤ Some men go for complete all-over smoothness, achieving the 'last chicken in the shop' look. Never, ever do this

-30
POINTS

SITTING DOWN TO PEE

Being able to stand and pee is one of manhood's great advantages. Any man who sits down is surrendering his dignity and piddling away his man points. Men, quite literally, need to take a stand.

➤ Claims that you get to read if you sit down to pee are just propaganda. The average pee is only about 25 seconds. So unless you have a bladder problem, you're not going to get much reading done

➤ If men start to sit to pee, sports stadiums and pubs will have to be redesigned. What if every man at Wembley decided he needed to sit? The crowd would never come back after half-time

➤ Writing your name in pee on a wall aged 12 is a rite of passage. Sitting down to go will kill this off. Won't anyone think of the children?

-15

POINTS

HAVING
A BATH

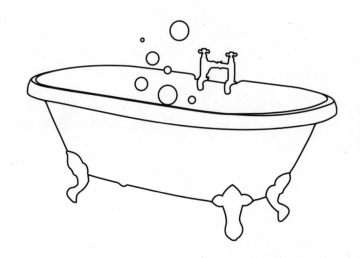

Having a bath is only manly if you are wearing a cowboy hat, smoking a cigar, have a bottle of bourbon in there with you and are getting regular buckets of fresh hot water brought in by a pretty saloon maid. Basically, if you are Clint Eastwood. All other solo baths are unmanly.

- Running yourself a bath is bad enough. Lighting candles and having bubbles only makes it worse

- Sports baths, even though taken with a bunch of naked men, are very manly indeed

- Joining your significant other in the bath is OK too. Just make sure that they understand that they have to go at the tap end

-25
POINTS

OWNING
STUFFED TOYS

It is a fine and manly thing to own a stuffed real animal: even better if it's something you personally have shot. But owning a teddy bear or cuddly-wuddly penguin is not good form.

➤ Having a teddy from childhood is not endearing. Any man who thinks it makes him interesting is right, in the same way Norman Bates was 'interesting'

➤ How would you feel if your friends knew you shared your bed with Mr Flopsy Bunnykins? They'd understand, right?

➤ It is OK to buy soft toys for your girlfriend, on the strict understanding that, after purchase, you only ever touch them to mop up spilt beer

DRINKING
FRUITY DRINKS

Fruit-based drinks are sweet and colourful, and about a million miles away from the manly drinks of beer and whisky. Put it this way: how comfortable would you be ordering a pina colada or strawberry daiquiri for yourself in a crowded pub full of other men?

- No man should ever be seen holding anything with an umbrella, straw or sparkler. Red, green and blue drinks all lose man points

- Respect the noble pint. No man ever turned to another and said, 'Do you fancy a melon martini in the pub after work?'

- Red wine is the only acceptable fruit-based drink, but only at home, not in the pub

-20
POINTS

OWNING PATTERNED WELLIES

Owning wellies at all strays dangerously close to breaking the three-shoes rule, but if you must own a pair then they should be regulation black, or dark green at a push. Colours, patterns and furry linings are forbidden.

➤ Would your grandfather recognise them as gumboots? If they pass this test, your wellies are OK

➤ Patterned wellies can be a symptom of manly decay: colourful umbrellas and novelty ties are other telltale signs that man-rot has set in

➤ Wellies are functional. Would you buy patterned toilet paper? Exactly!

-25
POINTS

ENJOYING ROMCOMS

Every man will have suffered through at least one romcom, and come away understanding that these films aren't intended for them. But if you found yourself really caring about whether Ryan Gosling and Reese Witherspoon did get back together, then there is something deeply wrong my friend.

> Talking about a romcom with other men is not possible. Men's film discussions are extremely simplistic: 'I liked it when his head came off', etc. Imagine talking about *Love Actually* with your mates. And shudder

> If you're compelled to go to the cinema by your girlfriend to see a romcom, use it as an opportunity to catch up on some sleep, or take an iPad with a real film preloaded

> To tell whether a film is a romcom, try this simple test. If the plot can be summarised thusly: 'couple meet in quirky circumstances. Complications ensue', then it definitely is and you definitely shouldn't

-40

POINTS

CRYING AT THE NOTEBOOK

If you are unfamiliar, *The Notebook* is a film undoubtedly written by a focus group of emotionally incontinent weepy-junkies about young lovers thwarted to only reunite in old age and then die together, with which many women are bafflingly obsessed. Many men have, in fact, cried after watching *The Notebook*: running out of the room clawing at their eyes in horror at what they have just seen.

> This film is designed and intended to make people cry. Self-respecting men must not

> The correct emotion to feel after watching it is rage – that you will never get those two hours back

> Friends don't let friends watch *The Notebook*. Knowingly allowing an unsuspecting buddy to watch it also loses you man points

POINTS

BRINGING A BAG ON A NIGHT OUT

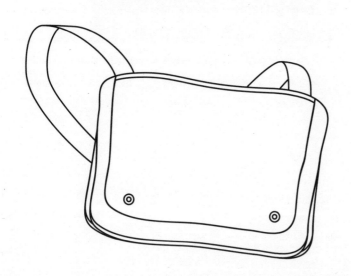

Getting ready to go out is a pretty simple task for most men. A sniff test will tell you if a shower is required, followed by a quick check to see if a coat is needed (i.e. is there a blizzard?). That's it. No dancing about to upbeat pop or trying on different outfits. And certainly no bag. The holy trinity of wallet/keys/phone are all you need, and they fit in a pocket.

➤ Taking a bag down the pub on a Friday night is only permissible if it contains your military kit, and you plan on being deployed directly from the King's Head to Afghanistan at closing time

➤ Bringing a bag shows a level of pre-planning. This loses points. The best nights out are partly adventures into the unknown

➤ If you take your bag to a nightclub, there is a very real chance that you'll end up dancing round it, with heavy points loss resulting (see p119)

-50
POINTS

BEING A
VEGETARIAN

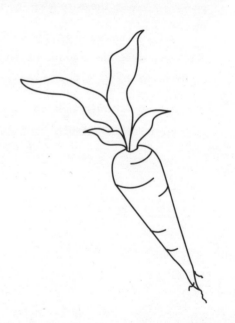

Man and meat go together, like sausage wrapped in bacon. Anything that upsets this natural order is deviant and unnatural. Therefore, most vegetarians are pale creatures with a weak handshake, who probably don't like beer or monster trucks. Nil points.

➤ Being a vegetarian isn't even very hardcore. At least you can sort of admire vegans for the extremity of their beliefs

➤ Don't fall for the reverse psychology that being a vegetarian is manly because it takes balls to go against the crowd. Vegetarians were never in the crowd in the first place

➤ As in nature, so in men. Lion vs gazelle. Fox vs hare. The lesson here is that carnivores always win

SLEEPING WITH
THE LIGHT ON

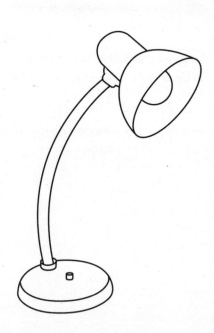

Asking mummy to leave the door open at bedtime was OK when you were a child. But a full-grown man has no business checking under the bed for monsters and being frightened of the dark. The dark should be afraid of you.

- The exceptions to this rule is, of course, the unavoidable situation of falling asleep drunk and waking with all the lights in the house blazing and the telly on

- No grown man should face the bed-wetter's paradox: do you wait until it's light to go for a pee because you're scared of getting up in the dark, or risk wetting the bed?

- It is your job and your job alone to investigate strange noises in the house at night. See p44

-30 POINTS

OWNING A HAIRDRYER

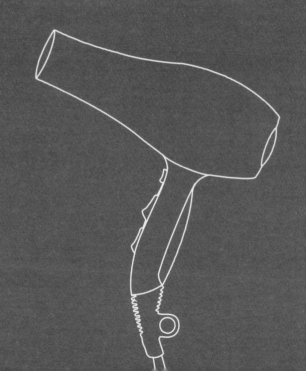

Scientific studies have shown that a short back and sides should take approximately 10 to 15 minutes to dry naturally at room temperature. There is absolutely no reason to own any sort of hair drying or styling gizmo at all. If your hair needs a helping hand, a spin in your open-top sports car should do the trick.

➤ Did your mum tell you that going outside with wet hair would give you a cold? Well it won't

➤ Hairdryers are noisy. Do you really want to announce to everyone within earshot that you're standing in front of the mirror giving it the full Vidal Sassoon?

➤ Using a hairdryer is the first step on a slippery slope to excessive grooming

POINTS

BUYING FLOWERS AS A ROMANTIC GESTURE

As all right-thinking men would agree, the romantic buying of flowers is utterly pointless. Flowers should be essentially viewed as currency: buy them to get you out of trouble, because you want to get laid, or as a reward for bringing forth your sprog. Any man who buys flowers because 'they smell nice' needs to have a long and serious talk with himself.

- Never be the bloke who buys a red rose in a restaurant: you don't need to give the waiters another reason to spit in your dinner

- If you have to have flowers, know that the ones from the man who sells them at the roadside don't smell of roses, but petrol. Schoolboy error

- As any botanist will tell you, giving flowers is actually giving someone a severed sexual organ. Just saying

-20
POINTS

USING FABRIC CONDITIONER

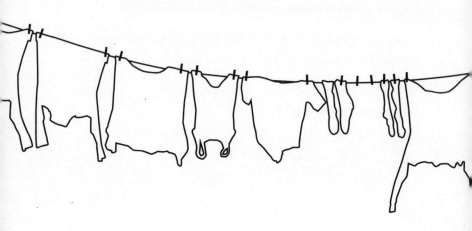

Chain mail. Scratchy army uniforms. Chafing rugby shirts. This is manly attire, where the harsh rub of material on skin is all part of the essential experience. Only softies want soft clothes. Real men like it rough.

➤ Think of the pictures on fabric conditioner bottles. Is it men splitting logs? No. It's women and children, frolicking in meadows

➤ Make like a monk in a hair shirt. Itchy, uncomfortable undergarments are good for your soul

➤ Fabric conditioner is a gateway drug. Before long you'll be moisturising and own a foot spa

-25 POINTS

HAVING THE WRONG PET

Tiger, bear, pig. Mike Tyson, Ivan the Terrible, Winston Churchill. Proper manly pets and their owners. Note that this list does not include: cats, rabbits, ponies, guinea pigs or hamsters. If you own a dog, it must be longer than your forearm.

➤ Never succumb to the idea that it's a good idea to carry your pet in a manbag. It's not

➤ What you name your pet is vital. Fang, Jezebel or Titan are good. Any names that begin 'Mr' are not acceptable

➤ Remember you are the master. Should you find yourself cancelling a trip to the local because you don't want to leave your cat alone, it's time to consider a pet-free life

POINTS

GOSSIPING

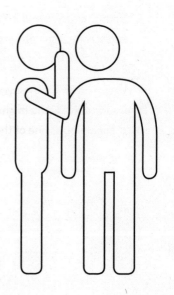

Careless talk costs lives, and men gossiping costs man points. In management terms, gossiping isn't one of men's core competencies. They lack fundamental interest in other people's lives, and a memory for detail that is the petrol in title tattle's engine.

- The only gossip it is acceptable to partake in is football transfer rumour speculation

- Knowing what is and isn't gossip isn't tricky. Talking about a friend's sports injury isn't gossip: speculating about whether this affects his ability to satisfy his girlfriend is

- Gossiping will not get you far with the ladies. Or, at least, not in the way you want. You might get to sit with the girls, but only because they think of you as one of them

MAN POINTS SCORE SHEET

LIGHTING A FIRE WITHOUT MATCHES	35
UNBLOCKING A DRAIN	30
SWIMMING OUTDOORS IN THE WINTER	40
BREAKING DOWN A DOOR	40
GUTTING AN ANIMAL	35
BUILDING FLAT-PACK FURNITURE	25
READING A MAP	20
CARVING MEAT	20
CONQUERING A MOUNTAIN	30
DRINKING YOURSELF SOBER	50
PUTTING UP A SHELF	30
EMPTYING A MOUSETRAP	20
WIRING A PLUG	20
EATING VERY SPICY FOOD	20
APPREHENDING A CRIMINAL	50
TAKING A PUNCH	30
CHECKING OUT NOISES AT NIGHT	25
PLAYING SPORT WITH A HANGOVER	15
SAILING A WATERBORNE CRAFT	35

BREWING YOUR OWN BEER	30		FIRING A GUN	40
PARKING	10		TYING A BOW TIE	15
DRINKING ALL NIGHT	45		EATING OLD FOOD	25
ORDERING DINNER FOR SOMEONE ELSE	35		DIAGNOSING ENGINE TROUBLE	30
BUILDING A SHED	50		DEMOLISHING SOMETHING	55
EATING MEAT	5		NOT GOING TO THE DOCTOR	15
GETTING A TABLE IN A BOOKED-OUT RESTAURANT	25		GETTING OUT OF A SKID	45
DRINKING NEAT WHISKY	15		CARRYING HEAVY THINGS	30
HITCH-HIKING	40		REMAINING A BACHELOR	45
BUILDING A RAFT	50		DEALING WITH AN ANGRY ANIMAL	40
BUYING DIY STUFF	30		GIVING A SPEECH	35
HUGGING (DONE RIGHT)	15		FLYING A PLANE	60
RIDING A MOTORBIKE	40		SMOKING A CIGAR	35
TRAVELLING LIGHT	25			
CHOPPING WOOD	40			
SHOPPING FOR CLOTHES (DONE RIGHT)	20			
WET SHAVING	10			
HAVING A SCAR	15			
WHITTLING	20			

ANTI-MAN POINTS SCORE SHEET

BEING IN TOUCH WITH YOUR FEELINGS	-25
DANCING WITH BOTH HANDS IN THE AIR	-30
HAVING A RUBBISH HANDSHAKE	-35
NOT KNOWING HOW TO RIDE A BIKE	-50
GOING ON A SLEEPOVER	-40
SHARING AN UMBRELLA	-20
BEING SCARED OF SPIDERS	-35
READING INSTRUCTIONS	-45
OWNING MORE THAN THREE PAIRS OF SHOES	-15
WEARING JORTS	-30
SMELLING WRONG	-10
GOING TO A HAIRDRESSER	-30
KNOWING THE CHARACTERS IN SEX AND THE CITY	-INFINITE
DOING YOGA	-20
BEING SCARED OF POWER TOOLS	-30
MANSCAPING	-40
SITTING DOWN TO PEE	-30
HAVING A BATH	-15
OWNING STUFFED TOYS	-25

DRINKING FRUITY DRINKS	-20	
OWNING PATTERNED WELLIES	-20	
ENJOYING ROMCOMS	-25	
CRYING AT THE NOTEBOOK	-40	
BRINGING A BAG ON A NIGHT OUT	-25	
BEING A VEGETARIAN	-50	
SLEEPING WITH THE LIGHTS ON	-20	
OWNING A HAIRDRYER	-30	
BUYING FLOWERS AS A ROMANTIC GESTURE	-25	
USING FABRIC CONDITIONER	-20	
HAVING THE WRONG PET	-25	
GOSSIPING	-35	

TOTAL MAN POINTS	
TOTAL ANTI-MAN POINTS	
GRAND TOTAL	

MAN QUIZ

NEED TO ASSESS YOUR MANLINESS IN A HURRY? USE THIS QUICK QUIZ.

1) In poker, which is the best hand?

a) Four aces and a king

b) A full house

c) A royal flush

2) What does an Ironman event involve?

a) Swimming, running, cycling

b) Drinking, curry, gambling

c) Dancing, talking, crying

3) Who was the best James Bond?

4) Do you own Speedos?

5) You're attacked by a dog. What should you do?

a) Run away

b) Wrap your arm in a coat and shove it down the dog's throat

c) Drop to all fours and start barking

6) What does a 'spa break' involve?

7) In which film will you find Travis Bickle?

8) Which of these is the best destination for a stag night?

a) Paris

b) Las Vegas

c) Brighton

9) Who scored the winning goal at Wembley 1966?

10) What is Polaris?

a) The North Star, vital for night navigation

b) A type of fancy sunglasses

c) A nightclub in Sweden

11) Do you moisturise?

a) Yes, I use a moisturiser as part of my beauty regime

b) I do occasionally use my girlfriend's face cream when she's not looking

c) Kebab grease running down my chin gives my skin all the help it needs

12) In the context of soft furnishings, what purpose is served by a throw?

13) Shark, lion, hippo. Which is the deadliest animal to humans?

14) What is the motto of the SAS?

a) Just Do It

b) Who Dares Wins

c) Because You're Worth It

15) How long does it take you to grow a beard (in hours)?

16) Have you ever seen *Frozen*?

17) What is testosterone?

a) An Italian sports car

b) A hormone essential for masculinity

c) A type of triangular Swiss chocolate

18) What are the minimum requirements for making a fire?

19) In your car boot is there more likely to be:

a) A set of golf clubs

b) The body of your enemy

c) ABBA's Greatest Hits

20) Have you ever cried in another man's arms?

21) A chicane is:

a) An Ibiza dance act from the 1990s

b) A series of bends on a motor racing circuit

c) A natty walking stick

22) How many men does it take to change a light bulb?

MAN QUIZ ANSWERS

1) C

2) A

3) Sean Connery

4) Unless you are a professional swimmer, no

5) B

6) Trick question: you should not know this

7) *Taxi Driver*

8) B

9) Geoff Hurst (both the controversial third goal and the famous 'they think it's all over' goal)

10) A

11) C

12) No known purpose

13) Hippo (they kill more than 300 people a year. A lion manages 200. Sharks only a pathetic 20 kills a year)

14) B

15) The answer should be less than 48

16) No, of course not

17) B

18) Tinder and a spark

19) A (or B if you are in the Mafia)

20) No (unless it was at the culmination of a particularly fraught sporting occasion)

21) B

22) One, so long as someone tells him where the light bulbs are kept

HOW DID YOU SCORE?

| 18–22 POINTS | 11–17 POINTS | 0–10 POINTS |

You are all man, an alpha male. If you aren't already, go and have a steak and a beer to celebrate

Good effort. You're pretty manly. A few weeks hard living every year should keep you on track

You need to man up, fast. In a survival situation, you would be first to be eaten. A programme of red meat, whisky and shed building is urgently required

ABOUT THE AUTHOR

Jonathan Swan is an expert on manliness. He lives in a shed in North London, cooks only over an open fire and has never knowingly eaten a quiche or a cupcake.